DEAF CULTURE
Our Way

DEAF CULTURE
Our Way

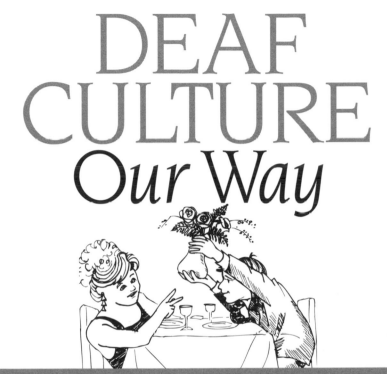

Anecdotes from the Deaf Community

By ROY K. HOLCOMB, SAMUEL K. HOLCOMB, and THOMAS K. HOLCOMB

FOURTH EDITION

DAWNSIGNPRESS

San Diego, California

Deaf Culture Our Way

Illustrations by Frank Allen Paul and Valerie Nelson-Metlay
Manufactured in the United States of America
Published by DawnSignPress

Library of Congress Control Number: 2011920798

ISBN-13: 978-1-58121-149-8

First edition published in 1977 as *Hazards of Deafness*.
Second edition published in 1985 as *Silence is Golden, Sometimes*.
Third edition published in 1994 as *Deaf Culture Our Way*.

10   9   8   7   6   5   4   3

ATTENTION

Quantity discounts for schools and bookstores are available.

For information, please contact:

DawnSignPress

6130 Nancy Ridge Drive
San Diego, CA 92121
858-768-0428 VP • 858-625-0600 V • 858-625-2336 FAX

www.dawnsign.com

Contents

Foreword

We have personally known the authors Roy, Sam, and Tom long before Roy's book "Hazards of Deafness" was published. We are honored that Tom and Sam invited us to write the foreword for the fourth edition of this book.

This book is a great way to introduce deaf culture's way to new parents of deaf children, students in the fields of deaf education and interpreting, new friends of deaf people, and anyone who enjoys a good story.

Many of the anecdotes remind us of our own experiences growing up deaf…Alan with deaf parents and Vicki with a hearing family. Adding to the mix are our deaf and hard-of-hearing children and hearing grandchildren. This book is a reflection of the unique experiences that deaf people have in a bicultural world.

Education, community service, and advocacy have long been a passion of ours so we expect this book to not only introduce deaf culture to folks but also to allow deaf people to enjoy reflecting on their own experiences as they read through it.

T. ALAN HURWITZ AND VICKI T. HURWITZ
PRESIDENT/FIRST LADY
GALLAUDET UNIVERSITY

Introduction

The original version of this book, by Roy K. Holcomb, was entitled **Hazards of Deafness** and was published in 1977. That publication was considered a breakthrough in the study of Deaf culture because it was the first to present the unique way of life among deaf people through their own eyes. A total of 662 compiled vignettes portrayed humorous, hazardous, and sometimes embarrassing experiences of being deaf in a predominantly sound-based world.

In response to popular demand, a new edition, **Silence Is Golden, Sometimes**, was published in 1985 in a condensed form for easier reading. Specific categories were developed to organize the "hazards" into groups such as traveling, dining out, communicating and mainstreaming. This version proved to be even more popular, selling out completely far before anticipated!

In 1994, Roy K. Holcomb's two sons, Sam and Tom, worked together to prepare the third edition of the book. The name of the book was changed to **Deaf Culture, Our Way** to capture the growing interest among deaf and hearing people alike in the fascinating culture of deaf people. Additional categories were created with a focus on contemporary hazards resulting from new technology. Those additions, along with classic deaf jokes and hilarious bathroom tales, made the book even more entertaining and enlightening.

Because Deaf culture continues to be influenced by the advent of new technological devices, the Holcomb brothers have teamed up once again to update the book to reflect the changing nature of the deaf experience. The fourth edition of **Deaf Culture, Our Way** includes new categories on pagers, videophones, video relay service, and e-mail/instant messaging, none of which existed when the third edition was published in 1994.

In addition, with a growing interest in examining the experiences of hearing people who were raised in deaf households, better known as children of deaf adults (CODAs), a section has been added to describe their experiences of having to balance between their deaf life at home and the hearing world at large. Additionally, Deaf culture is often thrown in the way of hearing parents who unexpectedly find themselves with a deaf child. Anecdotes of their experiences dealing with Deaf culture are also included.

Have fun exploring the wonderful world of Deaf culture from the eyes of Deaf people and the people who live with them.

ROY K. HOLCOMB, SAMUEL K. HOLCOMB, AND THOMAS K. HOLCOMB

Classic Humor

The following jokes have been passed down through generations of deaf people and are widely known among individuals within the American Deaf community. They are usually among the first to be shared with newcomers to the Deaf community. There may be as many versions as there are tellers; the following stories are presented in their basic forms.

KING KONG

On a hot summer day, many people were frolicking at a local beach until King Kong appeared on the scene. Seeing the huge ape, people began to scream and hustle off the beach, except for one lovely young lady. Unaware of all the commotion, the woman continued to sunbathe peacefully. Having scared everyone away, King Kong approached the only remaining person on the beach and scooped her up in his hands. She was frightened and began to scream. King Kong tried to tell her how beautiful she was. She indicated that she was deaf by pointing to her ears and shaking her head. King Kong was surprised to learn that she was deaf, because he knew some sign language. He began to sign, "You are so beautiful. I want to marry you." But in the process of signing "marry," King Kong smashed the girl into pieces.

HONEYMOON

A young deaf couple was driving down the road in a busy convention-filled city on their wedding night, looking for a room to celebrate their first night of matrimony. After finding the last available room in the entire town, the groom swooped the bride out of the car and carried her into the room. The groom was eager to begin their first night together, but the bride insisted on a bottle of champagne to make their wedding night complete. The groom grudgingly left and drove to an all-night store to buy a chilled bottle. When he came back to the motel, he could not remember in which room his bride was waiting, and the motel office was closed for the night. After a moment of pondering, he came up with a plan. He blared the horn of his car until the light of every room at the inn was turned on. Knowing that his wife could not hear the horn, he easily located his room—it was the only one with the lights out.

SIGNING COP

After picking up a hitchhiker on a lonely stretch of road, a deaf man was speeding down the highway. In a short while, a cop pulled him over. The hitchhiker felt bad for the deaf driver until it became apparent he was not going to receive a citation because he was deaf. The deaf driver smiled and sped away as soon as the cop was out of his sight. Later, he was stopped by yet another cop. Once again, he pretended to have much difficulty understanding the cop, and he was let go without a ticket. The hitchhiker was so impressed that he wanted to give it a try. By that time, the driver was getting tired, so he decided to let the hitchhiker drive for a while. The hitchhiker thought this would be his golden opportunity to drive as fast as he wanted without getting a ticket. Sure enough, a cop pulled him over after clocking him at 100 miles per hour. The hitchhiker started to play deaf and acted as if he could not understand the officer. The cop started to sign, "So you are deaf. I have deaf parents. Please give me your driver's license." The hitchhiker was dumbfounded.

ROLL CALL

At many residential schools, it is customary for personal belongings to be labeled with students' names to prevent them from getting lost. Often, young students who have difficulty remembering all the letters in their names will look at the label to help with the spelling. One day, a student proudly wore a new shirt he just got for his birthday. When it was his turn to spell his name during the roll call, he looked at the label of his shirt and quickly spelled "J.C. PENNEY."

HOLD THE JOB

A deaf man who worked in a print shop had the reputation of being the best printer around. One day, he had been holding a piece of paper for several hours. Finally, a co-worker asked him what he was doing and why he was not working. He replied that his boss had told him to hold this one.

DEAF TREE

A lumberjack was busy working in the forest, chopping down trees. A responsible lumberjack, he would yell "Timber" each time a tree was felled. One day he came upon a tree that would not fall, no matter how hard he chopped or how loudly he yelled. After consulting with his fellow lumberjacks, he decided to call a tree doctor. When the tree doctor examined the tree, his diagnosis was that the tree was deaf and could not hear the signal "Timber." The prescription was for the lumberjack to learn the manual alphabet. He mastered the alphabet and fingerspelled TIMBER to the tree. Lo and behold, the tree began to fall.

JOB HUNTING

An unemployed deaf man read in the newspaper about several job openings with a company. He went into the main office of the company, wrote something on a piece of paper, and gave it to the secretary. The secretary said "No, no, no" and sent him to the person above her. After reading the paper, that person also referred him to someone at a higher level. Finally, the deaf man was brought into the president's office. The president, after reading the paper, wrote "No, I want to keep my job." What the deaf person had written on the piece of paper was "I want your job" instead of "I want a job."

CAN YOU READ?

After observing a deaf person in a public place, a hearing man decided to approach him and find out whether deaf people are literate. He wrote "Can you read?" and handed the note to the deaf person. Disgusted with the man's ignorance, the deaf person wrote back, "No. Can you write?"

RAILROAD CROSSING

A deaf man was driving in the country and came to a railroad crossing with the gates down. After waiting for a while with no train in sight, he became impatient. He looked around and saw a small gatehouse by the tracks. He got out of the car and approached the gatehouse. Inside the gatehouse was a man dozing off. The deaf man knocked on the door and asked for a pencil and paper. In an attempt to communicate his need, he wrote a quick note. The gatekeeper looked down and saw "PLEASE BUT" and could not figure out what the deaf man was trying to say. He didn't know that the sign for "gates opening" looks like the sign for "but."

THE INVISIBLE HANDICAP

A hearing man was fascinated with a deaf woman who was sitting in a bar. He decided to strike up a conversation with her by writing notes on a piece of paper. To his delight, she was friendly enough to write back. They wrote back and forth for some time. Another man jumped into the conversation and began to write too. All three continued their conversation by writing. After a while, the deaf woman realized she was late for a commitment and told her new friends that she needed to leave. The two men waved good-bye and continued to write, not realizing that neither one of them was deaf.

OUR CULTURE

Deaf people have a unique culture, one that is based on sight rather than sound. Consequently, our way of behaving and thinking usually revolves around sight. This collection provides a glimpse of how deaf people function in a society dependent on sound.

You go to a movie theater with a group of friends. In the middle of the movie, you need to go to the restroom. Upon your return, you cannot find your seat. You stand for a few moments and look for heads that are constantly shifting toward each other. You start heading in that direction because you know they are your friends—only deaf people would sign to each other constantly throughout the movie as they try to help each other figure out the plot of the movie without captions. Even with captions, deaf people often compare notes throughout a movie.

You usually walk facing traffic to keep everything within your eyesight.

You call a friend. You let the phone ring more than ten times because you know that it is possible for your friend to be home but not see the lights flash.

When waiting in a busy doctor's office, you sit in a strategic location where you can easily lipread the caller and be as visible as possible so that you will not miss your turn.

You are confused about whether people can hear bodily noises. You just can't figure out when the grumblings in your stomach are loud enough for people to hear.

You are a dedicated parent who wants your young child to learn the English words for various objects in the house. You put signs all over the house with the correct word for each object. One day, you forget to turn off the stove after using it. You decide to make a sign with the word "STOVE" on it and put it on the kitchen door to help you remember to turn off the stove each time you leave the kitchen. Your child sees the sign and says, "No, no, wrong, wrong, it's not a stove, it's a door."

When running downstairs to put clothes in the dryer, you also grab your infant to keep her within your sight. Otherwise, the house could become a wreck during your few minutes of absence.

You get ready to leave a party. You find yourself actually leaving an hour later, finishing up conversations here and there and making plans for the next visit.

Unlike your hearing peers, you finish all your responsibilities and duties at work quickly due to lack of verbal distractions. However, when you take a long break, you get reprimanded.

When inserting coins in a soda machine, you put your hand on the machine to feel the coins drop before making the selection. Experience tells you that the machine won't cooperate until the coins have dropped completely.

To prevent forgetting to turn off the stove fan, you automatically turn on the stove light as a reminder that the fan is on.

You feel the dashboard of your brand-new car to make sure it has started.

In response to new parents of a deaf infant who ask you whether you felt cheated by your deafness, you say no, but the oral education you received cheated you.

You are getting ready to fly on a commuter plane to a small town. You realize that there is only one gate for eight different commuter planes. You don't know whether the line forming at the gate is for the flight you want. You approach the line and peek at the destination on the tickets people are holding in their hands to make sure you don't get on the wrong plane.

When introducing a friend, you quickly provide the person's background information, including hearing status, school background, affiliations with organizations, and names of mutual friends. As if this chunk of information is not sufficient, names of old flames are often given too!

When visiting a deaf friend at his home, you go through a specific routine if there is no answer at the door. First, you ring the doorbell long enough to make sure there is no possibility that your friend overlooked the lights. Then you check the door to see whether it is unlocked. If it's locked, you walk around the building and take a look through the windows and in the yard. If it is unlocked, you ring the doorbell once again before entering. You flick the hallway light and continue your entry into the living room. After all these fail, you write a note. Otherwise, your friend will accuse you of not waiting long enough or trying hard enough to make sure he is not home.

You change your doorbell light system to a cordless one. Now the chime goes off before the light flashes. Often hearing people press the doorbell button just enough to hear the chime, but not long enough to activate the light system. You find yourself writing a note on the door, asking people to hold the button for several seconds.

In order not to miss your bus, you must keep your eyes riveted on the street while everyone else casually walks around, reads, or carries on a conversation.

When someone asks you a question you don't want to answer, you just smile, gesture "I can't hear," and walk out.

Driving a car while carrying on a conversation in sign language can be tricky. As a passenger, you share the responsibility by keeping your eyes on the road and alerting the driver of any possible obstacles. That way, the driver feels more confident in maintaining the conversation for a longer period of time.

Thanks to laws assuring your right to have an interpreter in the emergency room, it may take longer to receive medical attention. You may have to wait for the interpreter to show up instead of the good old-fashioned method of using paper and pencil to communicate with the medical staff.

You get into a fight with a friend. She gets tired of fighting and locks herself in a room. You are determined to get the last word in, so you write a note and pass it under the door.

You tap your friend on the shoulder to get his attention. After talking with him, you turn around to talk with another friend. You realize you forgot to ask the first friend something, so you turn around to tap once again and are surprised to find a different person who happened to step in at that moment.

You are chatting with a friend as you walk down a busy sidewalk. You alert each other whenever you approach a possible obstacle such as a post or fire hydrant. Otherwise you run the risk of getting injured.

You are discussing a hot topic. You begin to get emotional and sign furiously. All of a sudden, you knock your glasses off your head. The discussion comes to an abrupt halt while you look for your glasses, clean them up, and put them back on. Now the topic is not as hot anymore.

You go to a restaurant with a friend. The first thing you do after being seated is to remove the centerpiece so that you have an unobstructed view of your friends' hands.

When picking a restaurant, you choose the one with the best lighting. A poorly lit restaurant can make it difficult to carry on a conversation.

Despite all the advancements made in technology, you still need to have the lights on to communicate with your spouse in bed.

You dream in signs.

BATHROOM TALES

Among deaf people, privacy is assumed when you are not visible to others. For example, behind closed doors, it is safe to think that you have complete privacy. What you can't see, you don't know. It is often difficult for deaf people to imagine how sounds can carry through walls or realize how far they can travel even with doors closed. For this reason, many stories have been shared about awkward experiences in bathrooms.

You are appalled to learn that practically every sound can be heard through most bathroom doors. You are uncomfortable at the thought of people knowing whether you had a full bladder or a severe case of diarrhea.

You are never sure whether it is appropriate to pass gas in a public restroom when there are others in the room.

You are amazed that there is unwritten bathroom etiquette. You learn of this when your close friend, who happens to be hearing, alerts you to the fact that you make too much noise when you "take a leak" in the public restroom. Apparently, you were aiming for the pool of water, which produced a splashing sound, as opposed to a quieter, more polite stream against the urinal wall. You are even more disturbed because you thought you were minding your own business in a private stall.

At a social gathering, you announce to your friends that you need to go to the BATHROOM instead of quietly leaving the room or using a line such as "I need to powder my nose."

You are on a long flight. You need to go to the lavatory. You find a vacant one. You open the door and find someone there with his pants down. You don't know who is more shocked, you or the guy who forgot to lock the door.

You are in a restroom at your doctor's office to fill a urine sample cup. The nurse knocks on the door to see whether anyone is in the restroom to let a different person in. You do not hear the knock and are caught in an embarrassing pose.

You need to go to the bathroom in the middle of the night. You waltz into the bathroom and are surprised to see your mother-in-law sitting on the toilet. You do not know who is more embarrassed, you or your mother-in-law.

You are minding your own business in a bathroom stall. You feel someone knocking on the side of the stall. Then you see a hand waving under the divider. You are unsure what is going on. You hurry and finish. As you leave your stall, you receive a dirty look. You do not realize the person was trying to let you know that there was no toilet paper in her stall.

You are uncertain whether your bodily noises can be heard by others.

You, as a gentleman, walk into a public restroom and lock yourself in a stall. A cleaning lady comes in the room after calling to see whether anyone was in the room. You come out of the stall and rush out, thinking you were in the women's restroom by mistake.

While you are taking a shower, some friends drop by to visit and your wife lets them in without telling you. You walk from the bathroom to the bedroom, giving your guests a real burlesque show.

Classic Hazards

These hazards are excerpted from
Silence Is Golden, **Sometimes** and
are among the most popular ones from the
original **Hazards of Deafness**.

TRAVEL AND TRANSPORTATION

Driving in a car full of hearing buddies, everyone is laughing and telling jokes. You are the driver and don't dare take your eyes off the road to "listen," so you miss out. Later, you ask your friends to repeat the jokes, but they either have forgotten them or tell them in a condensed way, and the jokes don't seem to be funny at all. This also happens when there is a hearing driver in a car full of deaf buddies.

At the airport, everyone is waiting for the boarding call. Finally, they announce that people in first class can now board the plane, to be followed by business class passengers. Only then can ticket holders in Zone 1 board. Holding a Zone 1 ticket, you assume you can board with the first group. The man at the boarding gate wonders what kind of trick you are trying to pull when you approach the gate with the first class passengers.

On the plane, you are seated next to a blind man. Your speech is unintelligible. He keeps talking and you keep nodding, making for an unusual conversation.

At a full-service gas station, the attendant asks whether you want him to "fill 'er up," and you reply "yes." Then he asks whether you want him to check the oil, and you reply "yes." "Water?" "Yes." Then he says something you don't quite catch, but it has something to do with tires and so you assume he wants to check the air. You reply "yes," hoping he hasn't just asked whether you want four new tires or want to buy his filling station so he can retire.

En route to California the plane runs into trouble and is rerouted to Las Vegas. After the plane lands, the passengers are let out for a two-hour wait. Because you didn't hear the announcement, you are quite surprised to see how much California has changed with all the slot machines and casinos.

Unbeknownst to you, your muffler has a hole in it. You drive along obliviously. Imagine your embarrassment when you get a fine for disturbing the peace.

Driving in your car and minding your own business, you notice people passing and pointing fingers at you. Assuming they are merely making fun of your old car, you drive on, only to find later that your tailpipe has fallen loose and is completely disintegrated because it has been dragged along the road so long.

A pebble gets caught in your hubcap and you drive 800 clanky miles before someone brings it to your attention.

Finally you arrive at your destination and check into your hotel. On the first sight-seeing tour, much to your dismay, there are CDs that have been prepared to explain interesting facts about the beautiful place you are visiting and tour guides who speak from behind a microphone, preventing you from understanding one bit.

A flight attendant comes down the aisle and asks whether you would like something to drink. You want anything except Coke, but it is the only drink you can pronounce clearly enough to be understood. Guess what you end up drinking?

You start your car but don't feel the vibration because the motor is running so smoothly. You turn the key again and step on the gas, making so much noise that it sounds like a jet taking off. Passersby give you strange looks.

You are driving down the interstate and the radio broadcaster announces that all cars on that road should use alternate routes to avoid a long wait. You blithely continue down the highway and end up wishing all the while that the highway department had the sense to put up a flashing warning sign.

At a stoplight your car dies. You don't realize it until the light changes and you attempt to go. By the time you get your car started the light is red again and there is a long line of impatient drivers. You are thankful you are the only one who knows you are deaf.

Your car is hit by a hearing person's car. You want to call the police especially because you feel you are entirely innocent, but the hearing person refuses to call and leaves after exchanging the necessary information with you. There are no witnesses. You drive to the police station to report the accident but it is inconclusive who was at fault because there were no police officers or witnesses at the scene. This makes it difficult to collect from the other party's insurance company.

You buy a car with a built-in radio and because you have some residual hearing, as most deaf people do, you turn up the radio to hear it. One day a hearing friend is riding with you and you ask him whether he likes the music. "What music?" he says. All he can hear is very loud static!

DINING OUT

A typical meal at a coffee shop might go something like this: You are with a deaf friend, communicating in ASL. Every time you raise your fingers to sign, the waitress comes running. But when you really want something, she is nowhere to be found. She brings your order. You have ordered a ham and cheese sandwich but get a hamburger. She asks you whether you want more coffee and you say no because your cup is almost full. Later she asks what you think is the same question. You do want more and say yes. You discover as she removes your cup that the question she asked was, "Are you finished with your coffee?"

One night you decide to dine in a fine restaurant, and you wait in line with others. The hostess asks whether there are any parties of one who would like to be seated. When you get to the front of the line, the hostess asks how many and you reply "one." She gives you a look of annoyance, but you can't figure out why.

You smack your lips while eating and then wonder why all at once everyone is looking in your direction.

Because you have pretty good speech, when eating out with friends you usually do the ordering and talking with the waitress. Guess who gets the check every time?

A man at the table next to you asks whether he can borrow your sugar, but you ignore him because you didn't hear. He scowls at you as if you are very rude.

In college, you are a popular guy, athletic and well dressed. No problem with the girls. So one night on a date you decide to go somewhere really special. You take her to a high-class restaurant, acting very suave and debonair. You open the door for her and seat her at the table in a manner Sir Walter Raleigh could not have improved upon. Then when the waiter comes, your date has to do the ordering because even though you went to an exclusive oral school, you can't say "potatoes" clearly enough to be understood.

One night you have a craving for a fast-food hamburger, and you rehearse exactly what to say so that they won't ask you too many questions. You tell them what you want on it and that it is "to go" and you give them the exact amount of money. Then, feeling satisfied with yourself, you stand quietly and wait for your hamburger. However, the employee seems to be waiting for something else, so you repeat your order carefully. Finally she waves her arms, motioning for you to move so that she can wait on the people behind you.

In a classy restaurant with a group of friends you are approached by a woman carrying a camera. She asks you several questions you can't really understand, but you assume she wants to take your picture for a fee. You have no desire to do this, so you shake your head every time she asks you something, trying hard to discourage her. After she leaves, one of the hearing people at the table is laughing his head off. He tells you that the photographer had said these things:

Boy, do you people look sharp tonight?
Bet you are going to paint the town red!
Are you from out of town? (You are.)
Isn't it a beautiful evening?
Would you like your picture taken as a courtesy of the house?

DEAF CONSUMERS

Waiting at a pharmacy to get a prescription filled, you decide to do some shopping to pass the time. When you finish, you check back, but it isn't up on the "ready" shelf. So you do some more shopping and check back again. Still no prescription. Finally you ask what happened and find out your prescription was put under the counter when no one answered the page on the loudspeaker.

When you take things out of your pocket, many times other things come out and fall on the floor, which you don't realize until much later when you are missing something.

A typical scene in a drugstore when the numbers on the cash register are not visible: The clerk says $3.30, and you interpret $3.13. He says $3.40, and you think it's $3.14 and so on.

In the grocery store doing your weekly shopping you are studying the different sizes to get the most for your money. A woman with a cart says "pardon me," but you don't hear and don't budge. She gets so frustrated that she slams into your cart and stomps past in a huff, when all she needed to do was tap you on the shoulder.

You are doing some shopping and up ahead you notice some people moving their hands. You assume that they are deaf. Upon getting closer, you find they are not; they were gesturing to make a point.

Buying a pack of gum seems like a simple enough task, but not always. You think the clerk said 90 cents, so you put 90 cents on the counter and head toward the door. Suddenly everyone is looking at you, and the clerk is having a fit. After much ado, you realize the clerk said 96 cents, not 90 cents.

Making a small purchase with a twenty-dollar bill can be unwise if you walk out without getting your change. You are halfway to China before some nice, honest person catches up with you and gives you your change.

In a store it is often necessary to take a number and wait your turn. This is an awkward procedure for deaf people. You must watch the person with the number just before yours and shadow him better than Sherlock Holmes could have.

MISUNDERSTANDINGS

Slamming a door usually means the person is angry, but when the look on your face is a smile, this is confusing to the hearing person.

You often drag your feet when you walk because it's a habit, not because you enjoy annoying people.

Smoking a pipe is one of your habits. One day a pretty girl gives you the eye while you are smoking, and you imagine she thinks you're quite handsome and debonair. Later, a friend confides to you that you make a terrible sucking noise while smoking, and you don't feel quite as debonair.

Watching television, you turn up the volume to hear a little, until the tenants down the hall come running in, telling you they can hear your television better than their own.

You are playing cards with a bunch of hearing buddies, and someone tells you that the noisy way you shuffle the cards drives them crazy. You end up winning the game, even though this tactic was not part of your strategy.

One day in a supermarket, you accidentally and unknowingly knock over a display of canned vegetables. You continue on your merry way and wonder why everyone is glaring at you.

Sipping your drink through a straw, especially when the glass is almost empty, can annoy a lot of people.

You brush your teeth and gargle before bed each night. One night your mother comes running in and asks, "What's the matter? It sounds like you're choking!"

You walk into a meeting in session oblivious to the fact that you're making all kinds of racket and causing the speaker to lose his place.

On a camping weekend you end up sleeping in your car because the campsites are all full. During the night, your leg leans against the horn and soon everyone in the entire camp is up looking around. Some are even banging on your window. You get angry for being awakened at 3 AM for no reason at all.

COMMUNICATING

Your brothers and sisters always liked to eavesdrop on your parents and you played along too, thinking it was great fun even though you couldn't hear a thing.

Your mother is telling you and your brother and sister something very exciting, as you can see from their expressions, but you can't understand. She later repeats the information but not with the original enthusiasm and excitement. You wonder what the big deal was.

You orally tell a friend to meet you at the Acme supermarket at 10 AM. She misunderstands you and goes to the A&P. When you see each other again she accuses you of having the world's worst speech, and you accuse her of not being able to lipread worth five cents.

You start feeling sorry for yourself because no one has visited you for more than two weeks. Then you find out your flashing doorbell light has burned out.

As a child you often played in the yard while your father did the gardening or other chores. One day he is repairing the roof and tries to get your attention, but you are not looking in his direction. To draw your attention in some way, no matter how crazy, he puts on a show on the roof that would rival prime-time television.

You are staying in a motel where they will serve you breakfast in your room if you call for it the night before. You aren't informed of this until morning, when you spend a long time trying to let them know that you want breakfast in your room without having to go to the front desk and tell them in person. By then you might as well have had breakfast in the coffee shop.

A hearing friend tells you she is going to bowl. When someone asks for her, you tell them she went bowling. Later, someone tells you she was boating, not bowling. Finally you find out she actually went to vote.

You happen to be with a hearing person and are talking, carrying on a conversation. As he talks he looks in another direction and you look too, thinking something important is going on. You continue talking and this time he looks in another direction. Then it dawns on you that hearing people sometimes look away while talking because they don't need to lipread and don't realize how important eye contact is to deaf people.

You tell a "deaf" joke to a group of hearing people. They laugh but don't understand it. They tell you one of their jokes. You laugh but don't understand it. You tell another one. They tell another one. Kindness can be carried too far sometimes.

When arguing with a deaf friend who decides to shut his eyes and stop "listening," you have to figure out how to get him to open his eyes so you can finish your argument.

You and your wife, who is also deaf, are watching television together. She moves. You think she wants something. You look in her direction. You move. She thinks you want something. You both move, and you both think the other person wants something. Later, you move to get her attention. She doesn't see you. Then she moves to get your attention, and you don't see her. Then you both move at the same time and both look. You both start talking at the same time. You both stop talking. You invite your wife to talk first. She talks. Then you talk. You go back to watching television. You move. Your wife thinks you want something.

You lost a hundred bucks at the racetrack and are trying to think of a way to tell your wife the bad news. When you come home she is in the kitchen cutting up some meat with a butcher knife. You decide that this is not the right time to tell her—she might, in a fit of anger, start signing with the knife in her hand. Later her hands are busy with knitting and you decide this is the right time because she will have to put down her knitting to talk back.

In a large crowd of people you have spotted a friend. You wave frantically, hoping she will see you, but she looks away the moment you wave. You realize you probably look like a fool, so you pretend to be scratching your head.

You are talking orally with a deaf person who was never allowed to learn sign language. Neither of you can lipread very well and although you both have interesting things to say, neither of you can understand a word.

In a dark movie theater, you suddenly want to tell your friend something. If telepathy really worked, it would certainly come in handy here.

Lipreading a person with a foreign accent is apt to make you think your eyes are out of focus.

Your speech is good enough to get by when talking in person, but the telephone is another story—you can't hear well enough to understand the conversation on the other end. One day you ask a stranger to make a call for you from a phone booth. He dials the number and hands the phone back to you.

Few people realize that lipreading a person with a moustache is like hearing half a conversation.

A person you meet tells you that you are a very good lipreader, and you reply, "What did you say?"

You demonstrate your lipreading abilities to the world: A guy says Wednesday and you think he said "windy." He says Thursday and you think he said "thirsty" so you invite him to a bar for a drink.

One day as you're walking down a street, a policeman blows his whistle at you to stop. Unaware, you continue on your way. Later you are thankful you did not get your brains blown out as has happened to other less fortunate deaf people.

While you're in the bathtub the phone light flashes, and you don't see it. Later, you're in the bathroom again, and the phone light flashes again. You decide to clean your closet, and the phone light flashes. Your friends ask you later where you've been all day, and you reply that you've been at home, wishing someone would call.

You are looking for some friends at a convention in a small hotel. At the desk, the clerk tells you they are in room 486. You move heaven and earth to find 486 in a three-story building and finally return to the clerk and ask her to write it on paper. Then you learn something: "4 and 6" looks like "486" on the lips.

Party and group situations are prime places for miscommunications with so many people talking, often at the same time. While everyone is chatting, you find yourself struggling to keep up so you laugh with the others when they laugh, frown when they frown. Soon you grow weary of this acting and decide to be yourself. Then you begin to think of something particularly funny that happened recently and smile to yourself and let out a chuckle. Everyone looks at you as if you are crazy because they are talking about a friend's serious illness.

Your friend's little girl is trying desperately to tell you something. You realize what she wanted after she wets her pants.

One disadvantage to being deaf is that other people who use sign language can "eavesdrop" from afar. You discover this after spending a two-hour lunch gossiping with a friend about everyone you know. Then you look up and spot a friend in the balcony who has seen your every word.

A local radio station is sponsoring a contest with a prize of $1,000. Every day someone's phone rings. If the person gets the question right, they get the prize money. One day the question pertains to Christopher Columbus. You happen to be an expert on Christopher Columbus, knowing everything from the number of times he kissed Queen Isabella's hand to the number of birds that flew over his ship while he was on his voyage to the new world. Your phone rings. You try to answer it on your teletypewriter (TTY). No answer. No $1,000.

While riding on a bus, you need to ask the driver for some specific directions. He answers you while looking straight ahead. You realize the only way you're going to be able to lipread him is to get on the hood and look through the windshield.

A friend has asked you to help him move some of his furniture. You are trying to move a large, heavy sofa down a flight of stairs. He takes the front and you take the rear. He is going a little too fast for you but is looking in the opposite direction, so you can't do much except hope his insurance is paid up.

You and a friend are walking down a street engrossed in a signed conversation, so much so that you don't see the woman coming with a large sack of groceries. You collide, spilling cans and boxes everywhere.

MYTHS

Sometimes people become deaf because of spinal meningitis. This is what happened in your case, and because of the meningitis, your balance is poor and your walking is uneven. One night you have the misfortune of encountering a policeman who thinks you are intoxicated and hauls you off to jail. Unable to communicate, you stay there until morning when your wife comes to pick you up. Only then do they realize you are deaf, not a drunk.

Deaf teachers often have to deal with parents who don't want their children in their class. They assume deaf teachers cannot be good teachers because they can't speak or teach speech. Ironically, the child grows up wanting to be a teacher of the deaf.

You apply for a job where a deaf person was fired for being a slow worker. The employer assumes all deaf people are slow workers so you don't get the job, even though you have a reputation of being a fast, effective worker. You wonder how many other employers are prejudiced.

Frequently, there are rumors about a miracle cure for deafness. As a prominent figure of the deaf community, you visit schools and organizations of the deaf all around the country. Oddly enough, you have yet to encounter one of these people who has miraculously regained his or her hearing.

When you are at a mall, you often notice people moving their hands and you assume they are deaf. You are puzzled when you discover they are not. This happens time and time again. Then you learn that hearing people use their hands when communicating, too. You wonder why back in school you were told not to use your hands for communication, although this was what you needed them for the most.

A doctor thought he had the perfect solution to deafness: Stop deaf people from having children. Then someone told him that this was all well and good but that only 5 to 10 percent of deafness is inherited and that a better way to do away with deafness is to stop hearing people from having children. The doctor lost his interest in doing away with deafness.

MAINSTREAMING

An accident of some sort has occurred on a busy street, and people have gathered into a large crowd. You ask a woman what happened, but you don't understand what she says. You pull out your pad and pencil and hand it to her. She walks away, thinking you are a reporter or a pest.

Many people go out of their way to avoid deaf people. They don't want to come in contact with you at all, as if being deaf were contagious. You can't help wondering whether their attitude is contagious.

Playing hide-and-seek as a child was always a fun game. You had to be very careful not to make noise that the hearing children could hear. You would find such a good place that no one found you and wait there for ages. Then you would discover that the game had ended long ago.

Every once in a while you happen to turn around just as someone calls your name, leading them to believe that you are not deaf after all. What hearing people don't realize is that deaf people will often look around just to make sure everything is okay.

Sometimes a hearing person will ask you whether you know a specific word. Usually it's a simple word even a child would know. So you find it easier if you play along and say "no," and let him elaborately explain it as if he were doing his scout duty for the day.

One of your "helpful" neighbors treats you as if you are helpless. She buys you groceries, volunteers to make your phone calls, scolds your children, and even gets after your husband when he misbehaves. She drops in at any time without ringing the bell until she finds you. If your lights don't come on at night, she is over to make sure everything is all right. She knows more about you than you know about yourself. But she has just one flaw—she loves to gossip. The entire neighborhood knows your every habit.

When talking with a hearing person, the conversation usually goes fine until another hearing person comes along and you are dropped cold. Then one of your deaf friends comes along, so you talk with him. Then the hearing person feels left out.

You have been invited to a friend's home for a family dinner. When it's time to say grace they all bow their heads. Because you have no idea when grace is finished, you become an expert at looking out of the corner of your eye, watching for the heads to come up again.

Applauding as an audience member is a simple thing, unless the applause has ceased and you are the only one clapping.

You're at the horse race and your favorite rider is winning race after race. You get ready for the kill and put a hundred dollars on him to win. They announce a change in riders, and your horse and rider come in fourth. You wonder what happened.

You have enrolled in a class and have to drive 60 miles every week to attend. You have no interpreter, but you make out by taking notes from classmates. One week, as class is breaking up, the instructor announces that there will be no class the following week. The next week you drive sixty miles and wonder what happened when no one shows up.

At a meeting with an interpreter a question is directed to you. Everyone in the room has to wait until the question is relayed to you. Just hope you get the question right the first time.

A well-meaning friend drags you to the opera. Once there, you find yourself watching the tails of the pianist, examining the dental work of the singers, and counting the number of people dozing off.

Even when understanding nothing, you nod and act as though you do, continuing to listen to what the other person is saying. They too will nod their heads when you talk, though they too understand little. What actors we all try to be!

As a young boy in a public school, recess was your favorite time of the day. One day when it was time to be dismissed, the teacher let only the girls go first. How embarrassed you were when you found yourself standing in line with them!

Walking past the neighbor's house, you almost get your leg bitten off by the neighbor's dog you didn't notice growling. You continue on your way, oblivious to the fact that the dog is following you, still growling. You are daydreaming about going to the National Association of the Deaf convention when all of a sudden you feel teeth in your leg.

You remember one time in school, as the star football player, how you took the ball through the middle, throwing opponents left and right, and you ran 70 yards for a touchdown. Then you found out the whistle was blown 20 yards back where a clipping penalty occurred. Moments of glory are often short-lived.

You are very surprised to find a bunch of neighbor kids in your child's room, hollering and playing cowboys and Indians. You wonder when your child let them in.

One night while you're driving your car, a policeman pulls you over for running a red light, which you are sure you did not do. He comes to your window and you reach for your pad. He reaches for his gun. If you try to talk he may think you are drunk. It's very frustrating to sit while an officer writes you a ticket for something you didn't do.

The television is on and across the screen flashes "Special Bulletin." You see the President's face and hope he is not announcing a nuclear war, but have to wait until the next captioned news program.

One morning you find yourself two hours late for work because your flashing alarm clock went off when your head was under your pillow and you did not see the alarm.

Usually at the parties you attend the deaf and the hearing mingle, trying hard to communicate with one another. But by the end of the night the hearing people are on one side of the room and the deaf are on the other.

You turn on the sprinkler to water the lawn and forget about it until the neighbor calls and tells you the ocean might run dry if you don't turn your water off soon.

Your block nearly burns down and every fire truck in the county is parked outside. You are inside sleeping the night away.

New Technology:
New Ways & New Hazards

Although new technology such as pagers, videophones, video relay service, video remote interpreting, e-mail, and instant messaging usually means enhanced life experiences for deaf people, they also have resulted in new hazards for deaf people.

HANDHELD DEVICES

Hand-held devices are a "must-have" technological gadget for many people. These devices provide deaf people with immediate access to their loved ones and friends. By the mid to late 90s pagers and mobile phones were becoming popular with deaf and hearing people. Although today more deaf and hearing people use the same devices, there are new sets of rules and challenges for deaf people to navigate.

You tell your deaf acquaintance to "page" you and your hearing acquaintance tells you to "text" her.

Instead of using a paper and pencil to place your order at a fast-food restaurant, you use your pager to type your order.

After being annoyed for years by hearing people who would interrupt a live conversation to answer the phone, you now are annoyed by deaf people who do the same with pagers.

When your pager vibrates, there is no way of knowing whether the incoming message is urgent because it is not possible to customize the vibrating signals. Hearing people can customize the ringtones so they can identify the caller.

Unreliable connections can be a source of frustration, especially when waiting outside in the freezing cold to be picked up by a friend. You do not have the luxury of using a public payphone as a backup.

You receive a page asking why you have not responded to an earlier message that was sent only two minutes ago. Messages sent via pagers are treated the same way as phone calls between hearing people; an immediate response is expected.

To communicate with your wife in another room, you page her.

The pager settings can be embarrassing. Instead of vibrating, the bell goes off without your knowledge. Even worse is unknowingly setting an "r-rated" song as the default setting.

You are locked out of your car and you left your pager inside the car. You have no way to contact AAA or your spouse or your friend for assistance. The public pay phone is of no use to you.

Because the system was down, you didn't get the message on your pager about picking up your spouse at the mall until the next day. You wonder why your spouse is mad at you.

When walking down the street, you are engrossed in your pager conversation, oblivious to the potential dangers around you such as road traffic, sirens, and people passing from behind.

Instead of using the doorbell, you page your friend to let him know of your arrival.

You've lost your pager but have no way to try and trace it, whereas hearing cell phone users can use another phone to call themselves and find their cell phone by listening for the ring.

You find yourself more concerned about protecting your pager from the nasty elements of the environment such as rain or snow, leaving your children to fend for themselves.

VIDEOPHONES

With the availability of videophones (VP), deaf people now can have instant communication with each other in ASL, even at a distance. Videophones are set up on a home's television set using high-speed connections and allow people to see each other when making phone calls. This has resulted in a completely different lifestyle for deaf people.

You just woke up from a nap to answer an incoming VP call, not realizing your perfect hairdo is not so perfect.

You can converse with anyone without worrying about your English skills. But then, if your ASL skills are not quite as good, you are at a disadvantage.

It is difficult to ignore an incoming VP call with its bright flashing lights.

While conversing on VP, you notice your messy home in the background. You are tempted to hold your conversation to tidy the room up a bit.

Every wrinkle on your face is captured on VP.

Your favorite TV show is interrupted by every incoming VP call, making it necessary to purchase a second TV set.

You can give a quick tour of your newly decorated room by moving the VP around the room.

You can ooh and ahh at your new grandchild through VP. You can also see your grandchild's first steps, first sign, and so on.

You can judge your daughter's new boyfriend by his looks and how he signs even if they live miles away.

With your new mobile VP, you make a list of all public spaces equipped with WIFI so you know where you can make a VP call in case of emergency.

With new mobile VP, you get funny looks from others when you make a VP call in a coffee shop. But then, you look as ridiculous as people talking to "themselves" using a hands-free phone.

Your ability to have a smooth conversation depends on the speed and quality of the bandwidth or connection.

VIDEO RELAY SERVICE

The Telephone Relay Service has now given way to Video Relay Services (VRS), improving deaf people's access to the hearing public. Instead of dealing with the slow, cumbersome transmission of information between the deaf TTY user and the relay operator who would read the typed message and translate it into spoken English for the hearing party, deaf people can now sign to the VRS interpreter and have their message instantly interpreted into spoken English. Even with this wonderful service, problems and frustrations exist.

The skill level of VRS interpreters varies a great deal, from native signers to less than fluent signers. It all depends on luck for what kind of interpreter will pop up on your screen.

You get confused when the VRS interpreter keeps referring to Sandy as a woman, while in fact Sandy is a dog.

Accustomed to the warm and friendly nature of communicating in Deaf culture, the cold and impersonal demeanor of VRS interpreters can be unsettling.

You tell your friend that you will be leaving Berkeley tomorrow to travel to San Diego and then on to Santa Fe to meet her. The VRS interpreter relays the message that you will be leaving Boston to travel to South Dakota and then on to San Francisco. You end up 1,000 miles apart.

Inexperienced with unsolicited sales calls from hearing marketers, you try to be polite and put up with the intrusion politely. You end up listening to a sales pitch for an hour.

You get a wonderful interpreter on VRS; you decide to make several calls to "keep" the interpreter.

Getting put on a long hold can be awkward with the interpreter staring at you.

Hearing "Hi, this is Mike" in a female voice can be confusing to hearing callers.

Long goodbyes famous in Deaf culture do not translate well in VRS calls. A smooth closure is not always assured.

Handling business through VRS is preferable to in-person transactions where there is no interpreter. This can be frustrating for the hearing person who needs to handle many incoming calls.

You have to deal with hang-ups frequently because the introduction made by video relay interpreters sounds very much like unsolicited business calls.

You do not realize long silences are uncomfortable for hearing callers.

You choose your VRS provider based on the size and shape of the monitor provided by the company.

You put on your best appearance as you make your call to your boss, forgetting that only the VRS interpreter will see you on the screen.

Ending a VRS-assisted call with an innocent I Love You sign can be confusing to the hearing caller if inappropriately and literally interpreted by the VRS interpreter.

You provide a crystal-clear description of the engine problem you've been experiencing with your car with your superb ASL skills. However, the video relay interpreter is unable to match your eloquence in English because of limited knowledge of auto mechanics and the limitations of English as a descriptive language.

You get confused when the VRS interpreter relays your hearing mother-in-law's message in a friendly manner while in fact you cannot stand each other.

You are rejected for long-term care insurance because you cannot be interviewed directly on the phone as policy prohibits third-party interviews.

You hesitate to provide your Social Security number through the VRS, even though it is required to receive appropriate service from certain offices.

VIDEO REMOTE INTERPRETING

The video remote interpreting (VRI) service is becoming increasingly available to address the chronic shortage of interpreters experienced by many communities. Many hospitals are now switching from using live interpreters to a remote service to assure the availability and immediacy of interpreting services. Instead of having a live interpreter in the room, you see the interpreter on a television screen, who might be thousands of miles away from you.

The placement of the TV monitor depends on the length of the cable instead of the optimal view from your bed.

You don't need to worry about being modest when being examined by the doctor because the interpreter is not in the room.

You are excited about the wonderful new technology because interpreters are supposedly immediately available 24/7 through a video service. However, you wait for an hour for the nurses to hook up the system and then try to figure out how it works.

Instead of having the interpreter move around the room to remain within your eyesight while the doctor attends to your problem, the nurse moves the TV monitor around the bed to keep the interpreter within your eyesight.

The regional signs used by the interpreter along with the pace of her signing do not match the typical signing style of deaf people in your area, making it difficult for you to follow the interpreter. Likewise, the accent and pace of the interpreter's voice make it sound like you are calling from an area far removed from where you live.

E-MAIL/INSTANT MESSAGING

Having access to e-mail has been said to be the greatest equalizer for deaf people in terms of access. Likewise, instant messaging (IM) allows deaf people to communicate with each other and with hearing people with ease. However, cultural differences can be confusing.

Signing off with a "hugs" or "xoxo" signals a warm closure that is typical among deaf people but can be confusing to the hearing recipient of your message.

Terminology that has become common in IM, such as LOL, has crept into sign language vocabulary, but not so for spoken English. This has made it awkward for sign language interpreters to find an appropriate English equivalent when you sign "LOL" in an interpreted meeting.

Blogging has given way to vlogging because it's much easier to sign than to type your messages. However, reading blogs is much quicker than watching vlogs.

Sending messages by e-mail is "slow" by today's standards. Sending messages via pager is preferable.

ASL terminology has also crept into IM language that makes no sense to those who are not familiar with ASL. ASL phrases such as "Dododo," "see-see," "kiss-fist," and "true-biz" are a quick way to communicate specific thoughts while using IM. These ASL phrases are quick and better substitutes for lengthier English phrases such as "What should we do?" or "What will you do about this?," "Let's see what will happen" or "I'll believe it when it happens," "I absolutely love it" or "This is totally my favorite," and "I'm serious about this" or "It is not a fabrication because it really happened!"

You forget that the rules associated with TTY usage such as "GA" for go ahead and "SK" for stop keying do not apply to IM chats.

Not So New Technology, Still a Hazard Today

Many advances in the area of technology do not always take into consideration the needs of deaf people. This collection demonstrates how dependent society is on sound, putting deaf people at a disadvantage.

UNSOUND TECHNOLOGY

You pull up to a self-service gas station. You proceed to pump gas in your car, unaware that the attendant had asked you over the loudspeaker to wait. You wonder why you get a dirty look when you approach the window.

You do not hear your clothes dryer beep at the end of the cycle. You find your clothes all wrinkled because you left them in the dryer far too long.

You find it frustrating to shop at stores where there are sophisticated computerized cash registers. Many of them do not have screen displays for customers, making it difficult for you to figure out the exact cost of your purchase.

You do not realize that machines have manners and voices nowadays. For example, when purchasing a can of Coke from a machine, it might say something like "Have a great COKE day."

You drive to a self-storage place to store your things. You find out that you must communicate through the intercom system to go through the gates. What makes it worse is having several cars behind you waiting for you to give the password.

You recently purchased top-of-the-line hearing aids. They are fully digitized and can be adjusted to fit your specific hearing needs. To your disappointment, people still give you a dirty look each time your aids whistle.

You are proud of your new expensive watch that has all the latest features. You can program it so that it will beep at specific times. Unfortunately, you never know when it beeps.

You are taping yourself doing an original poem in ASL about love and peace to be posted on YouTube. You do not realize the web camera is also picking up the sounds from your television on a special program about Pearl Harbor.

Even though you have installed an elaborate cordless doorbell light system, the pizza delivery person uses the knocker on the door. You wonder why your pizza has not been delivered.

Many cars now come with option packages that include fancy stereo systems. You have no choice but to pay a fortune for it if you want a well-equipped car.

You don't know whether the computer is processing the data after you push the save button. You resort to feeling the terminal to see whether the drive is running.

You rent a DVD to watch with your hearing date. After the movie, you stop the DVD before the closing credits begin. You do not realize that a popular romantic theme song was accompanying the credits. You lose a chance to be romantic with your date.

You just bought a new fancy personal computer. The only printed instruction that comes with your computer is "Congratulations! You have purchased the finest piece of technology in the world. Please listen to the CD for instructions on how to assemble and use the equipment."

You are driving in the country in the middle of the night. You need to withdraw some money from an ATM machine. The machine does not recognize your password and refuses to return your card. This message appears on the screen: "Please use the phone on your right and call for assistance." You are now stuck in the middle of nowhere with no cash.

Beep, beep, beep. You don't realize that you have pushed the wrong button and that the computer is trying to alert you to the fact.

You are not able to enjoy the convenience of the drive-through window at your favorite fast-food restaurant unless you have the audacity to get in the line, bypass the speaker, and drive up to the window to give your order. Sometimes you receive someone else's food.

The computer is down at your company. The last time it was down, it took two hours before it came back on. You loaf around, not realizing that the computer was repaired within five minutes and everyone is back to work except you.

You click on the remote key control several times to make sure the car doors are locked, driving your hearing friend crazy.

CLOSED-CAPTIONED TELEVISION

As recently as the late 1970s, deaf people were not able to enjoy television programs to their fullest because they were not captioned and much guessing was required to understand the dialogue. Today, almost all shows are captioned and the text appears on the screen with a special decoder built into the television set. Unfortunately, this technology is not without flaws.

Decoders are supersensitive to interference, such as the wind blowing, although the picture often remains clear. You swear every time the wind blows!

You are watching your favorite soap opera. The secret that you have been dying to find out all season long is about to be disclosed on this particular program. Just when the actress begins to blurt out the secret, an emergency bulletin about an upcoming hurricane comes on, blocking the captions.

You continue to record every program that is captioned. You have collections of shows that you have not yet watched. You find it difficult to break this habit because you remember when there were only ten hours of programs that were captioned each week. That made it necessary to tape shows to watch during nights when there were not captioned programs on television.

You buy a tiny new TV set. You realize you need a magnifying glass to read the captions.

Because you grew up without captions, you love watching TV now. You don't want to miss television shows for any reason. Your away message says "I'm busy watching TV now."

MURDER SUSPECT ROBERT
JOHNSON AGED 23

You are watching the evening news on TV. The top story is about a murder. You start laughing when the captions get behind the actual dialogue and a picture of an ape appears when the name of the suspect is finally given.

You feel that the local stations do a good job serving their deaf viewers by captioning their news programs. However, when a natural disaster hits your area, you are routinely left in the dark with no captioned emergency broadcasts.

You love watching local news shows on TV now that they are captioned. However, you continue to feel like a second-class citizen when the weather report comes on or when they go live with a special report, because these segments are rarely captioned.

Picking your favorite news show depends on which station does the best job captioning the program.

You pick a sports bar to watch the "big game" based on the willingness of the bartender to turn on the captions.

TELETYPEWRITERS (TTYs)

It was not until 1965 that deaf people were able to use the telephone. The TTY is a device that allows deaf people to use the telephone system, provided both persons on each end of the call have the device on their phones. A coupler was developed to be used with old TTYs from Western Union. Although TTYs are rapidly becoming obsolete, they continue to be used by some people who do not have access to videophones and pagers.

When it first came out, the TTY provided deaf people tremendous freedom and accessibility. It was a wonderful invention, except for one small shortcoming! It is impossible to interrupt on a TTY, so if you have the misfortune of talking to a long-winded person, you must learn to do other things like file your nails or make a shopping list while waiting for him to finish.

Your TTY is broken—and you can't use it to call a repair center.

During a power outage, you find you're the only one in the neighborhood unable to use the phone because TTYs depend on house electricity to operate.

You get a new TTY and find it to be defective. You call the sales department of the TTY company and receive an answering message: "Sorry, our TTY is broken right now..."

You tell your mother to send back her recently purchased TTY because you find it faster to talk with her through the relay service.

You are in the hospital. You are provided with a phone and TTY but no signal lights. You are limited to making outgoing calls!

You panic when the paper runs out in your TTY, knowing that you can't remember all the details of the gossip to share with your spouse.

White pages in the phone book now can indicate whether the listing is a TTY number. Now burglars have a way of knowing whether the resident is deaf.

When making a call on your TTY, you are used to two different light signals: long, slow flashes for a ring signal; short, rapid flashes for a busy signal. Nowadays, you get confused with different signals for fax, modem, voice mail, and all the other features that come with phones.

You receive prank calls through TTY and try to figure out who the caller is by the speed of typing, the choice of words, and the English grammar.

Because TTYs are expensive, you have only one. Instead of the luxury of having a phone in every room in the house, you find yourself running to the family room every time the phone rings to avoid missing calls.

You have a problem with the program on your computer. You use your TTY to call the computer expert at your company. Unlike your hearing co-workers, it is not possible for you to explain the problem while keeping your eyes on the computer screen. Rather, it is necessary for you to type the message on the TTY, look for your place on the computer screen, type again on the TTY, and so on, making the process slow.

You take your portable TTY on a trip. An emergency requires you to make a call, only to find the battery dead.

At the airport, you need to make a TTY call. You find a sign indicating the location of the phone with the TTY. You follow the sign to the phone only to find a hearing person occupying the telephone booth. You are frustrated that the hearing person just happened to use that particular phone to make a voice call, even though there are many other phones around the airport.

TELEPHONE RELAY SERVICE

The popular VRS has essentially replaced the telephone relay service as the most popular way to use the phone to access the hearing public. However, as long as deaf people continue to use their TTYs, the telephone relay service will continue to be an important part of the deaf culture experience.

You try to explain to a hearing person how to use the relay service. Sometimes you succeed. Sometimes you find it easier just to say, "I'll call you."

When placing an order over the phone, the process can become complicated because you need to give two sets of numbers, one for the relay service and one for the place you are calling from.

After receiving many busy signals, you finally get through to an airline office, only to receive a computerized answer instructing you to push certain numbers to reach the designated department. Because the relay operator could not type all the information in time, you get disconnected and start receiving busy signals all over again.

You call a number through the relay service. The person answering the phone says, "No, I'm not interested in your service," and hangs up. He does not realize that the phone call is placed through a relay service at no cost.

When you make a call through the relay service and receive an answering machine, more often than not the agent will need to type the message and then call again to leave the message. Sometimes, if the taped message is lengthy and rapid, the agent will need to call back just to be able to type the complete message for you.

Computerized answering machines that require you to push numbers to get the right department or person can drive relay operators up the wall.

A Hazard No More

Many hazards that were listed in the original *Hazards of Deafness* no longer exist, thanks to advancements in technology and enlightened sensitivity among people in today's society. The following collection is selected from the book, each with an explanation of why it is no longer a hazard.

You buy a TTY. You find your phone bill a lot higher than your neighbor's because you can't type as fast as they can talk.

Now you can call your friends anywhere for free with your VP.

In the hospital, you can't call your loved ones, but the bill collectors can't call you either.

Thanks to Section 504 of the Rehabilitation Act of 1973 and the Americans with Disabilities Act of 1990, hospitals are required to provide equal access to deaf patients, including the provision of TTYs. However, most deaf people now have pagers to keep in close contact with their loved ones.

An emergency news bulletin logo crosses your TV screen. Dialogue you cannot hear follows. You imagine all kinds of things happening, like Martians invading New York City. You must wait until you read the next day's paper to find out what really happened.

The law now mandates all emergency announcements on television be captioned.

You only half-close your car door and don't notice until you are on the freeway doing 80.

Now, with the light warning system on many cars, you are immediately alerted if the door is not closed correctly.

You wait all year for Santa Claus to come, and then when he does, you can't tell when he asks whether you have been good because his beard and whiskers make lipreading impossible.

It is now possible for you to tell Santa Claus that you have been good. Many places have special times for a signing Santa to make an appearance.

You spend half your life going to the post office to pick up or return captioned films.

Captioned films were a popular form of entertainment before television shows and movie rentals were captioned. Deaf people would often congregate at a friend's home to watch captioned films. Trips to the post office were frequent to pick up and return films.

You are an actress who gives a super performance that brings down the house, but you fail to hear one single word of praise or applause.

Visible applause such as handwaving is now popular.

Your tour group visits Washington, DC. You visit many historical places—the Washington Monument, the Lincoln and Jefferson Memorials, the Capitol, and many other sites. The guides are very busy explaining about each one. Because your tax dollars built them, you just wish that you could get a little more from your tax money by being able to understand what is said.

Interpreters are routinely provided for many tourist attractions with advance notice. You can now enjoy those national treasures as much as others.

You can't phone friends to wish them a happy birthday or invite them to a poker party. But then, no one can bother you when you're in the bathroom.

With pagers and hearing dogs, your solitude in the bathroom is no longer assured!

You watch a football game for ages wondering what the score is before it is finally flashed on the screen.

With captions on TV, you are able to enjoy the play-by-play comments by the TV sportscaster.

You apply for a job and have to impress your prospective employer with your looks and manners rather than the spoken word. Actions speak louder than words and it is possible to land something good if you play your cards right.

Thanks to the Americans with Disabilities Act (ADA), employers are not allowed to discriminate against deaf people. For example, an employer can provide an interpreter for the interview to ensure equal access.

You arrive at the airport to go to some far-off destination. You can't call your loved ones for a last farewell. You have to suffer in silence as you watch others make calls.

With a pager, you can have instant communication with your loved ones.

A friend who left her address book at home is passing through your city and has no way of locating you because you have no phone and your name is not listed in the telephone directory.

With technology such as e-mail and pagers, it is easy to keep in touch with your out-of-town friends.

You have a neighbor who loves to call your doctor for you. Soon the entire neighborhood knows your medical history and then some.

Privacy is now assured with the relay service.

You are called to jury duty. You state that you are deaf and are easily excused. You wonder what would happen if you accepted and showed up with an interpreter.

Deaf people are no longer automatically excused from jury duty. Interpreters are routinely provided.

You work in a factory and know every nut and bolt on every machine there. Your boss depends upon you for all the important jobs. However, when it comes time for promotions, you are quickly bypassed.

Thanks to the ADA and other federal laws and regulations, deaf people cannot be passed up for promotions just because they are deaf.

You ask a friend to make a call for you, never knowing that the message you wanted to give and what he or she actually said were as different as night and day.

Thanks to highly trained relay operators, your message is now being relayed precisely.

On a plane trip you have a one-hour stopover in Chicago. You have a lot of friends there but no one you can call on the telephone.

With VPs and pagers, there is no need to wait for stopovers to take advantage of free local phone calls.

Because you are deaf, all television programs, as well as movies, are "silents." You see more silents in a year than most people saw during the entire era of silent movies. Sad to say, most of your silents have no captions as well as no Charlie Chaplins.

Television programs are no longer "silent," thanks to captions on TV. However, movie theaters are not equally accessible.

You spend half of your life in airports waiting for late planes because you can't phone ahead to learn whether they are on schedule.

Thanks to the Web, you can access the information as easily as anyone else.

You drive 50 miles to visit a friend. You find he's not at home. You leave a note under his door stating that it is very important that he see you immediately. You drive the 50 miles back home. You find a note under your door from the same friend stating that it is very important that you see him immediately.

Your friends are now easily reached through pagers.

In the winter when snow is forecast, you can't listen to the school cancellations on the radio, so you wind up making the trip to school anyway.

Many television stations provide printed information about school closures. In addition, with captioned news program, you have the same access to information as your hearing friends.

While out on errands, you lose your bankbook. To find it, you have to backtrack to all the places you have been. If you could hear, you could phone the places you had visited and would not have to go out in the cold, snowy weather.

With the relay service, you can now call those places from your cozy home.

You look out your window and see a robbery under way but have no way of reporting it until it is all over and the robbers are in the next county.

Many police departments and 911 operators have TTYs in place, providing equal access to deaf people. Better yet, you can use your VP to call 911.

One day you have to make a phone call. You look for a person to help make your call. You find the person. You have to wait until the person is ready or able to do so. You complete your call. On another day you have to make another call. Again, you look for a person to make your call. You find the person. You have to wait until the person is ready or is able to make the call. On still another day you have to...and such is life with the phone.

With 24-hour relay service in place, you can make calls at your own convenience.

You and another deaf friend go to the University of Florida. You have no interpreter. Both of you get notes from different hearing friends. After class you compare your notes and find them so different that it seems that you had been listening to two different professors.

Interpreters are routinely provided by colleges and universities. At some places, notetakers are also assigned to deaf students.

You go to a convention on deaf education. Speaker after speaker tells how deaf children should be handled—and every one of the speakers is hearing. You wonder when there will be a convention on hearing at which every one of the speakers is deaf.

Total exclusion of deaf people from making contributions to the field is no longer tolerated. Deaf people are now sought after for keynote presentations and active participation in professional meetings.

You are at an airport and you miss your plane because you failed to hear the last call on the PA system.

Electronic boards near gates provide visible notices about departure times.

You take your chances in going to popular places to eat without reservations because you don't wish to bother people to call for you. Sometimes you get in, and sometimes you are turned away and end up eating at McDonald's.

Thanks to the relay service, reservations can be made at the restaurant of your choice—except for McDonald's, of course.

You never thrill to the phone call of a friend you haven't heard from for years or one who decides to call you from 3,000 miles away.

Easy access to information through the Web and Facebook gives you access to many of your friends, near and far.

You type away and don't hear the bell at the end of the carriage, so many of your words end up beyond your right margin stop.

Thanks to computers and automatic word wrap, there is no need to worry about the right margin endings of a typewriter.

You are on vacation. You leave loved ones at home and worry about them. You cannot call them, so you worry about them. Your vacation is half-spoiled by your not being able to be reassured that all is well at home.

Hotels are required to provide TTYs as well as decoders and flashing lights for smoke detectors and doorbells, thanks to the Americans with Disabilities Act (ADA). Better yet, your pager allows you to maintain close contact with your loved ones.

During the week, you are on cloud nine because you can watch the ABC captioned news if you live in the right part of the country. If you can survive the weekends when there is no captioned news, you can watch the captioned news every day of every weekday.

In most cities, every news program is captioned regardless of the day or time of the week.

You work at a newspaper plant. At every break, workers rush to the phone to call someone. You wish you could do the same.

Just like your hearing peers, you can use your pager or cell phone to make calls.

You arrive at your destination and then have to find a stranger to call for someone to come and pick you up. Often the stranger you ask will misunderstand you and point to the phone, where he expects you to help yourself. This is especially true when you have good speech.

Most airports now have TTYs available for deaf travelers to use. However, pagers are now the preferred way to communicate.

You buy a television set. You pay by check. The saleslady asks you for identification. She asks you for your phone number. You state that you don't have one. You purchase a car. The salesman asks for identification. He asks for your phone number. You purchase a home. The real estate people ask you for identification. They ask for your phone number. After a while, you start feeling sorry for yourself that you don't have a phone. You feel almost like getting a phone in your home to be able to say that you have one even if you can't hear or use it.

You don't need to buy a phone just to say that you have one. You can use the phone as well as anyone else with VPs.

Your parents give you their phone number at work to call in case of an emergency. One day an emergency occurs. You dial the emergency number you were given. You state your problem three times to be sure you get through, not knowing that the phone is busy on the other end.

With relay service, you can be assured clear and direct communication. No more hits or misses with emergencies.

A relative dies. Because of your inability to use the phone, you are usually the last one to know.

Many families now use pagers to keep in close contact.

You arrive at the airport after a trip. You can't call your spouse to come and pick you up, so you shell out close to a hundred bucks for a limousine to take you home.

Now all you need is a pager to let your spouse know of your arrival.

Your car begins to stall in the middle of the night on a freeway. You pull over to a call box on the side of the road. Finding yourself unable to use the phone, you are left stranded for a long time. Because of budget cutbacks, the highway patrol does not make routine rounds as often as it used to and responds to emergencies only when people call on the call box.

Pagers allow you to contact your family or friends for assistance.

You visit a hearing relative with your parents. You pray that she has a new television because all TV sets built after July 1993 are required to have built-in decoders.

Practically all TV sets are now captioned, making your trip to your grandma's more enjoyable.

As you travel through the country, you realize that the phone number for the telephone relay service differs from state to state, unlike the operator number (0) for hearing people.

Dialing 711 automatically connects you to a relay service operator.

You wait for your friend to call you back at a public pay phone. You keep your hand on the phone, waiting for it to ring.

Pagers/cell phones make public pay phones a thing of the past for deaf and hearing people alike.

Fax machines are definitely a blessing, but only if you can figure out the beeps. You have no way of knowing whether the line is busy because most fax machines do not have light signals for these beeps.

Fax machines are used less frequently. Instead, it is just as easy to send an e-mail with a scanned attachment.

Hearing People
with Deaf Parents

Hearing people who were raised in a deaf household have had to straddle two worlds: the deaf and the hearing worlds. Consequently, they experience the deaf culture first hand while growing up and, at the same time, function as hearing people. Anecdotes are provided below describing their unique place in the world.

You find yourself using the VP when calling your CODA friends so you can have a face-to-face conversation even if you communicate by voice.

You go to a hearing friend's house and find it difficult to enjoy a television show without turning on the captions, even though you can hear perfectly well.

You get frustrated when your hearing friend does not maintain full eye contact with you when carrying out a conversation.

Your hearing college roommate continues to chat away after the light is turned off at bedtime. You find yourself turning on the light to finish the conversation.

You find it distracting when your college roommate keeps the music on at all times. You are accustomed to a "quiet" environment.

No matter how old you are, you find yourself getting the bill at the restaurant because you were the only one who spoke when ordering food.

When explaining that your parents are deaf in an unsolicited phone conversation, the caller offers his condolences.

You can't understand why your hearing roommate gets annoyed when you inform him that you are going to the bathroom.

Out of habit, you sit in the front row to hear the presenter.

You find it necessary to inform your hearing roommates every time you return home, even though they can hear you.

While your roommate is on the phone, you ask who he is talking to, even though it might not be any of your business.

You find yourself signing to your friend even though she does not know any signs.

When an interpreter is working in a class you signed up for, you find yourself watching the interpreter to process the information even though you can hear very well.

You are oblivious to squeaky doors after growing up in a house full of squeaky noises.

You try to explain to your parents that birthday parties do not usually include parents.

You get frustrated when your hearing friend is ambiguous when providing feedback. You are used to direct and to-the-point criticism.

You wait until your teacher looks at you before answering her question.

You use typical ASL facial expressions such as nose-twitching or eyebrow-raising when conversing with your hearing, non-signing friends, which can be confusing or even offensive to them.

You incorporate ASL vocabulary such as "Pah" into your spoken English word bank, confusing your non-signing hearing friend.

You dream in signs.

Hearing Parents
of Deaf Children

Deaf culture can be new to parents raising deaf children and the cultural elements may remain long after the deaf child leaves home. The following snippets were shared by parents who have had the experience of raising deaf children.

You get used to the idea of deaf friends looking through the window to see whether your deaf child is home.

You give up after trying to teach your deaf child to be ultraquiet when going to the kitchen for a midnight snack.

You find yourself an expert in understanding deaf speech.

You get used to having deaf friends "overstay" at your house.

You feel sad for your child's deaf friend when he says how he wished he could communicate with his own parents.

You can't get over worrying about the safety of your deaf child even though he travels all over the world, rides on a motorcycle, plays football, and goes barhopping in the dangerous part of the city.

You get compliments all the time for how well you sign.

You find that your home becomes a comfortable place for deaf friends because you are one of the parents who can sign.

You get used to having bright lights in the house.

You find yourself happy for your deaf daughter when she tells you that your newborn grandchild is deaf.

You are adept in lipreading.

You can enunciate words so clearly that practically anyone can lipread you.

You dream in signs.

Blessings of Being Deaf

Being deaf can often be a blessing in disguise. Sometimes it makes everyday routines a bit more complicated but often it filters out some of life's annoyances and distractions.

You can enjoy a good nap anywhere, even in a noisy environment.

You don't have to worry about being awakened in the middle of the night by barking dogs or your neighbors having an argument or practically anything.

In the library you can communicate via sign language and still be quiet.

You don't have to write off your ears as a total loss. They can still be used for looks, to hold eyeglasses, to wear pierced earrings, and to balance your head.

You don't have to worry about loud music that your teenagers have blaring through the house. It won't make you deaf.

Watching television while your spouse is vacuuming the house does not bother you at all.

When walking down the street, you don't hear the catcalls made by obnoxious men.

You can congratulate a bowling friend several alleys down from you for making a strike.

There is no problem communicating through a window. This comes in handy when you are outdoors and wish to say something to someone indoors.

You go to bed one calm, starry night and awake to find that your home was almost blown away by a brutal storm that kept everyone else awake all night.

You don't have to worry about going deaf when you get old.

You are not easily frightened by squeaky floors or strange noises when you are at home alone.

About the Authors

Roy K. Holcomb is well known for his innovative work in the field of deaf education. He spearheaded several movements including the establishment of an international organization for parents of children who are deaf, known today as the American Society for Deaf Children; the widespread acceptance of the use of sign language in schools with young deaf children through the Total Communication philosophy; and the expansion of support services available for deaf children in mainstreamed settings. In addition, Roy broke the glass ceiling for deaf administrators by becoming one of the first deaf directors/superintendents in the nation (Sterck School for the Hearing Impaired in Delaware). He passed away in 1998.

Roy's oldest son, Sam, is best known for his work with ASL instruction. He has been teaching in the American Sign Language and Interpreting Education Department at the National Technical Institute for the Deaf at the Rochester Institute of Technology in New York since 1977. In 1983, he helped develop a series of sign language books, *Basic Sign Communication*. Again, in 2010, he was one of the co-authors of a new sign language curriculum, *ASL at Work*. He has conducted workshops nationwide on ASL instruction.

Tom, Roy's younger son, is a Professor at Ohlone College in Fremont, California, where he teaches courses related to Deaf Studies and Deaf Education. Previously, he taught at San Jose State University and National Technical Institute for the Deaf. Tom is well known for his innovative teaching materials on Deaf culture, including two DVD/workbook sets *A Sign of Respect: Strategies for Effective Deaf/Hearing Interactions* (2008) and *See What I Mean: Differences Between Deaf and Hearing Cultures* (2009), a training module on Deaf culture as part of the *Cultural Detective Series* (2006), and a textbook, *An Introduction to American Deaf Culture* (2012).